XOETEOX

WAVE BOOKS SEATTLE/NEW YORK

XOETEOX

< THE INFINITE | WORD OBJECT >

EDWIN **TORRES**

PUBLISHED BY WAVE BOOKS

WWW.WAVEPOETRY.COM

WAVE BOOKS TITLES ARE DISTRIBUTED TO THE TRADE BY

CONSORTIUM BOOK SALES AND DISTRIBUTION

PHONE: 800-283-3572 / SAN 631-760X

LIBRARY OF CONGRESS CATALOGING-IN-PUBLICATION DATA

NAMES: TORRES, EDWIN, 1958– AUTHOR.

TITLE: XOETEOX / EDWIN TORRES.

DESCRIPTION: FIRST EDITION. | SEATTLE : WAVE BOOKS, [2018]

IDENTIFIERS: LCCN 2018004693 | ISBN 9781940696737

(LIMITED EDITION HARDCOVER) | ISBN 9781940696744 (TRADE PBK.)

CLASSIFICATION: LCC PS3570.O696 A6 2018 | DDC 811/.54—DC23

LC RECORD AVAILABLE AT HTTPS://LCCN.LOC.GOV/2018004693

DESIGNED AND COMPOSED BY QUEMADURA

SLIPPAGES, TONE, ARSE POETICA DESIGNED BY EDWIN TORRES

PRINTED IN THE UNITED STATES OF AMERICA

9 8 7 6 5 4 3 2 1

FIRST EDITION

WAVE BOOKS 073

XOETEOX

A OTRO

imorta . . . sabilité

imorta . . . sabilimont

imorta . . . stámenémen

amenté . . .

amenté

aa orta

be otra

se otra

demonstro . . . stromonstro

eorca

fesolca

giganta

hesolp . . . hesolp . . . hesolpé mia

i orta

jazzaba sé be sé ba

kamonkro vi yabesa voltro me

lavisi livi lepe lomo

montrame moc mé como manqué ama mañana

nama nombre

o yorta osotra

pon ponto tworq ya

qua un qua un qui quaun ama

rasume namu

stressor sorro

tortorro rotoro

uorta

vevi vavo sortra

wwwwwwwwwwo xoxtra

xa men xa men xa melle sui amenté

ya yovorta

za mol tré

zzzzzzzza zol zzzzzzz

THE COLLAGIST AT THE EDGE

— the collected word object

— the collaged epic

— the realigned alpha-glyph

— the extracted real

— the glue brain

— the knowing of someone — anyone —

— near you

         why would I give you my thinking in bits

— so much space

         between thought/s

— separations

         between words, people,

objects — between — objects

         the between object

is every object, every edge

         is the one that decides — how to read

the one between

         all that control

forming combinations of all those edges

         all that *presentation*

— how do I want you to follow me, where will you go

         if you don't — should I worry

what will happen to me
        if my connections
misfire — my carefully crafted collage
       filtered
— into language

       the rough of my edges
smoothed down — by my hand
       with your ears
just out of reach, between landing
       and flight

          define the poet — as the one who loses themself — to the poem
              gain the poem — by finding yourself — in the poet
         the poet becoming the poem — is the human cycle — brought to language

a journey, made familiar
       by these sheets of grey and black markings
on white noise — *right here*
       in my hands
an act of understanding — a contract

       between you and me
a skin of cognition — a container
       holding us together —
your skin is incredibly porous
       your existence — unfolding within it

a journey leading back
            to its creation —
a *right now* — in the making
            that forms the beginning
of what you end — *right now*

            which began
way before you arrived — *right here* —
            why do I need you to get me
is the reason I need you to get me —
            to connect

and all your points of connection
            infinite and permeable
are where we start
            — *the collected word object*
            — *the glue brain*
            — *the cut heart*

TALISMAN

The object
that looks nothing like me
is the object that will probably kill me.

The blood cell
seeking the virus that looks nothing like the rest
will surround and terminate the danger.

The invention — is in the danger.

creativity redefines danger as creativity

culture redefines creativity as danger

who redefines danger redefines culture

The story of the boy and the clock, the lesson of the teacher and the boy,

the will of the boy and the world, the way of the world and the people,

the question of the people and the wall, the falling of the wall and the people,

the power of the people and the tweet, the alignment of the tweet and the twit,

the addiction of the twit and the screen, the worry of the parent and the screen,

the teaching of the planet and the dirt, the experiment of the flirt and the threat,

the melting of the climate and the neighbor, the color of the neighbor and the neighbor,

the construction of the ethos and the wave, the movement of the wave and the nation,

the home of the brave and the free, the scripture of the key and the lock,

the threat of the clock and the wires, the pyres of the higher and the lower,

the story of the globe and the boy, the freedom of the boy and the terror.

who redefines danger — redefines culture

TO THE TETRIC HEPTATHLETE

to the tetric heptathlete

we exist in a dialogue of existing
our ephemeral soil as divided as our tongue
the aural erasure that defines
our evolution in a *y thing* connection
the x crossing out the @ the o the y

in that crossing out a bridge
a new repository brought to light
where accent creates opportunity to shift
with the evershift — how to evolve
with the silent runners

TO THE RENDERED EXCISION

conforms to the fragment holding

knows its part holding its part

fragment holding fragment

they were all me I saw objects

in my *lower both* — inside the removal

— who is sacred to the word *sacred* —

is word part — the fragment spoken

— time holding both *calendar* and *both* —

is our living breathing both

TO READ WITH THE
SILENT RUNNERS

to sit with a book's silence

is to deepen the silence

to power a book's loudness with yours

        is to fuse your silence

        with a page — is to power

        your private world

to give yourself

silent power is to sit

with your silence weavers

        your fellow deepeners

        loudly with you

        inside

i leave my body

through sound i return

when i stop

        to keep moving

        when i sit with a spine

        of a book is deeper than knowing

if it is still a part of me

the next day

to offer the space to wake up

how we all have a bit of cave

inside

a hollow tone

bringing sound to the word

without answer

i look for an alternate tone

to find out what i'm missing

to *word* in my time

to go beyond the alternate say

THE STORY STORY

the size of each blade of grass had become bigger than a tree
oh, excuse me . . . I forgot . . .

one day . . .
there was a fox looking for his owl
or was that an owl looking for his fox

they were always playing games like that
I will make you as big as a skyscraper, said the owl
why are you scraping a sky, said the fox

I will fly over you as fast as a fox, said the fox
why are you flying over yourself, said the owl

wait a minute, what about the grass, why was it bigger than a tree
oh, excuse me . . . I forgot the story

one day . . .
a giraffe said hello to a fish
wait a minute, what happened to the owl, said a little girl

what little girl, said the fox
wait, are you telling the story now, said the storyteller
or am I, said a little boy

what little boy, said the tree

the fox, the owl, the giraffe, the fish, the little girl, the little boy, the tree, and the storyteller
all looked at each other

we need a cloud in this story, who said that
they all said, yes!

one day . . .
a cloud found a little frog
wait a minute, I want to know what happened to the giraffe, said the giraffe
the giraffe was saying hello to me, said the fish

hello
hello
how are you today
I'm a little wet
I'm a little tall
I'm a little ant
wait, how did a little ant get into this story
you call this a story
who said that

look over there, said the storyteller, a star is shining
but it's morning, said the monkey
how did a monkey get in here

what's going on fox
nothing much monkey, we're all sitting here
listening

ah it must be bedtime, said the flea
there's a flea in my soup, said the grass
grass can't talk, said the tree

everyone looked at the cloud

one day . . .
a moon was shining on a lake, said the tree
you can't see a moon in the day, said the ant
it must have been early in the morning, said the owl

owl, I have not heard from you since the beginning of the story, said the little girl
I know a lot about early in the morning, said the little boy
it must have been night, said the fox

is that when tree gets to be smaller than grass, said who

one night . . .
everyone was telling a story at the same time
a lot of friends gathered together
some starting to sleep, some just waking up

wait a minute, said the storyteller
does that mean that you are finishing the story, said the cow

what cow

ANATOMICALLY ERECT

in the ocean   someone is selling a doll with genitals — *a doll*
         as a boy made of genitals —
         the idea of   something called *boy*
                 who is not boy
                 but *genital* — words inflict, don't they

how gentle it sounds to say   *into the good night*
            go off tender boy
            go off your complete someone
made whole, by the doctor saying who you are — in the mom
            the first time we know — in the mom

is when the doctor — in the boy tells us who we are
         i was a baby until i was a boy
         i didn't know — what i had or didn't have
                until i was told
                i was a *gentle gentle* boy

kare kare in New Zealand   is a beach so powerful
         the Maoris   named it twice —
         kare is the Maori word for *stream*
            say say your *idea-dea*   and be strong
                 in the repetition of your say

your idea   hanging   between mine — *stream stream*
              ocean ocean   *poem poem*   *boy boy* — too strong
        for one name — the ritual passed
                          the indigenous offering blessed — to layer strength
over meaning, by naming it twice

in that repetition   the *repeated same* ignites
          — movement the *repeated same* ignites — movement —
                    first one *said* — then gone — *just said* — now gone
        second one   comes along — *inside* sound
                    of first one — there *there*

i just *just* said   *inside* first one
          — to make room —   for *same* shell
                          same vibration that i
        just *just* said   ignite move
                    ment — ibration — capapture — *kare kare*
        peni peni   *mony mony*   grips atoms   to make more

wave wave   *boy boy* — and his
          gentle gentle idea   someone had a thought
        to make a doll as *whole* as a boy
                    anatomical ocean
                    in a boy as *complete* as a doll — *plete*

assa dohl — the one piece   holding it all together

        so you can play with the thing

        that makes you whole — in one hand

                     closer

                     to what words can do

TONE

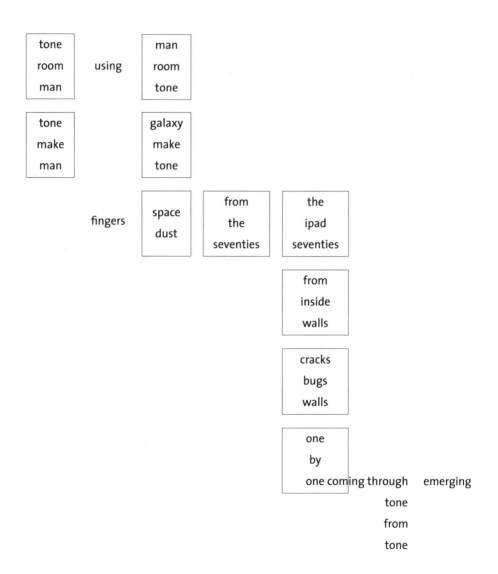

tone	using	man
room		room
man		tone

tone		galaxy
make		make
man		tone

fingers
space dust
from the seventies
the ipad seventies

from inside walls

cracks bugs walls

one by
one coming through   emerging
tone
from
tone

from nest to wall

from nest to world in wall

to hum outside

to world   of hummmmmmmmmmmmmmmmmmm

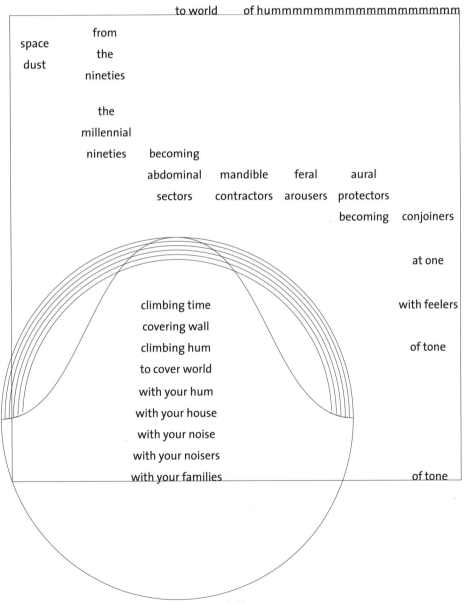

space   from

dust   the

    nineties

the

millennial

nineties   becoming

abdominal   mandible   feral   aural

sectors   contractors   arousers   protectors

becoming   conjoiners

at one

climbing time   with feelers

covering wall

climbing hum   of tone

to cover world

with your hum

with your house

with your noise

with your noisers

with your families   of tone

19

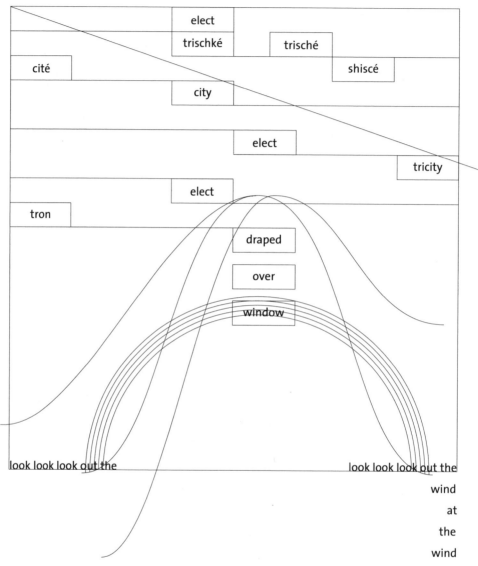

elect

trischké   trisché

cité   shiscé

city

elect

tricity

elect

tron

draped

over

window

look look look out the   look look look out the

wind

at

the

wind

the winnnnnnnnnnnnnnnnnnnnnnnnnnnnnnnnnnnnd

coming through   emerging

tone

from

tone

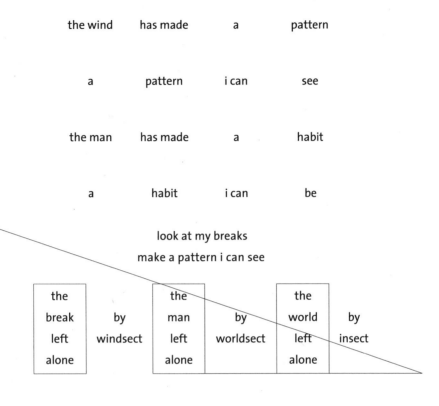

the wind   has made   a   pattern

a   pattern   i can   see

the man   has made   a   habit

a   habit   i can   be

look at my breaks
make a pattern i can see

the break left alone	by windsect	the man left alone	by worldsect	the world left alone	by insect

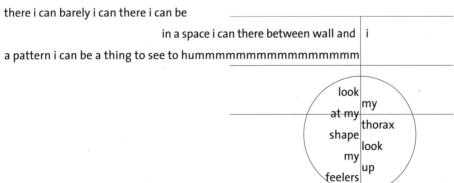

there i can barely i can there i can be

in a space i can there between wall and i

a pattern i can be a thing to see to hummmmmmmmmmmmmmmm

look
at my
shape
my
feelers

my
thorax
look
up
there   my sky

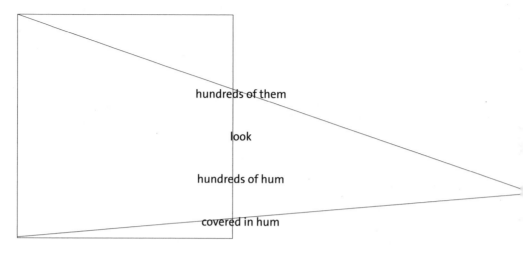

hundreds of them

look

hundreds of hum

covered in hum

my hauz made of

h u m m m m m m m m m m m m m m m m m m

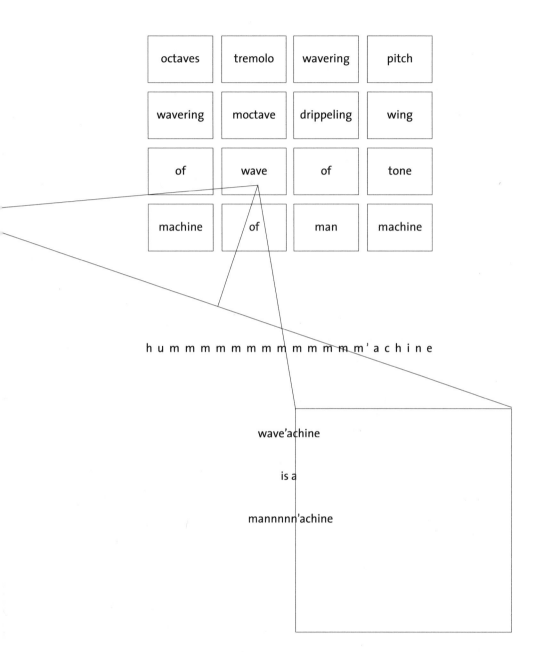

octaves	tremolo	wavering	pitch
wavering	moctave	drippeling	wing
of	wave	of	tone
machine	of	man	machine

h u m m m m m m m m m m m' a c h i n e

wave'achine

is a

mannnnn'achine

this man

made of tone

this hauz

now gone

this man

now gone

made of gone

mi voca

sacagone

mi luxe

meccagone

mi shatter

mattergone at the back of the throat of the gone   gone

the turn

gone

the man

to the moan

to the tone

alone

to the home

covered in home

the people to the gutter to the street to the room

look
look
in
here
the
man
out
there
the
page
not
here
the book

24

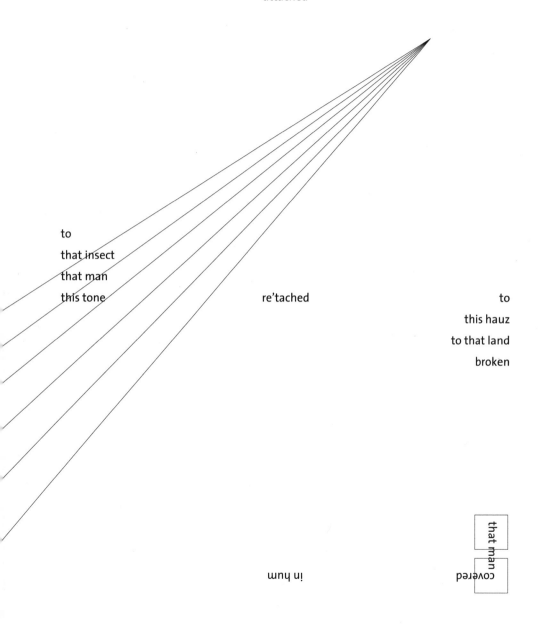

attached

to
that insect
that man
this tone   re'tached   to
                                              this hauz
                                            to that land
                                              broken

                          in hum   covered that man

OCEAN OBELISK

what is your gut telling you
the fleshed word at one with body
before edge if we to take
were to take our own fleshed indifference
and convey convert that
me to the opening w eim agine we
imagine to be would come we de
decipher the infiltrated edge
look at the smoothness we claim
as indifference a steady sameness
of our not belonging would that belonging
become any harder by hardly by edging
the flesh of our sometime arrival
our now arrival always an edge
the cover we slip into when we slip
under our heart our openings as ratchet
as our wounds our worlds our word

a cycle of lifetimes dedicated
to time's manifestation of time's slippage
under opening's underment of marvel
where surface obtains sewage
as centered obfuscation's mystery
paddling the incoherent applications
of myseriant fantasy the openings
cannibalize their own lifetime's
dedications being litmus to opening
made steadier by the realms of each
station each stop relegated to arrival
is the stop that slips under time
reared re-aired repaired in scrawl
by the hand that owns it there was
an owning at fire with its obelisk
a charged glow masked by ocean's
surface allowing the viewer entry
by opening its front stone to flesh in
that void the ocean speaking to sea

look at the pretty pictures my hands
can do my fingers my hands can do
my fingers if you look closely I can
breathe through my fingers I can if
you can can you breathe when you
look at my fingers when you look at
my pretty can you draw my pretty the
way I can the way my fingers get tired
get exhausted when I grip this pen too tite
tight don't forget the letter the speaking
of tiger in a hand world is important
to sell to spell how hard its world
is by saying tight not tite can you see
that titeness tight me in my experience
in my expressed hardness my difficulty
the world is showing the world is looking
when I draw pretty titeness almost as ugly
as the hand holding this titely DEFINED grip
did you see just there how I the hand claimer
capitalized what I thought was important how I draw
the most hardest word/world to make it pretty

excise my forget in the age of disdain for hubris
omnivert that omnivery for such a vacuous tone
on my eligible sanity
pardon sane the perv and his porosity to mail thyself
on slight when masking is jaundice vérité
volted on the tree of life the open sore is a long tooth
for good times excuse my martyred tragicomic impulse
to boheme the lifestyle for go! afire the stoppage
slippage being my forte, scrawl being my tool
hardness my lingering brevity a crafted excess
astutely male and generic, let my age be a misnomer
for the american dream shack my uncultured persona
a clichéd swipe at pregnant reasoning let
my exploned exp lanary overheard voyeuristic come-job
and splayer suburbia over the ear job you call commute,
excuse me while I martyr my backyard bachelorhood
into some orgasmic entrail gutted
by resolve succumb slack at life envy let me catch
the light again the one from obelisk craw that came to me
came when I expected east in guise of light opening
from a quiet state a state of meditative search disguised
as wave re-guised as body prone existented-istence-
tential-tense-ing-sintual

BLUE WHEEL RONDO

I let my blue wheels
lift life —
  come down the mountain

    come down the mountain

I let my blue wheels
gift light —
  turn down the mouth

    turn down the mouth

I gave my blue wheels
the gift of sight —
  let down the hum

    let down the hum

I gave my blue wheels
the lift of night —
  lay low lay lower

    lay lowest and low

I saved my blue wheels
a game of rain —
  come run the rounding

    come run the rounding

I thought my blue wheels
would want what I want — *what I want what I want*

    what I want what I want

I gave my blue wheels
a gift of life —   *turn run the byway*

                                              turn run the byway

I let my blue wheels
assist strife —   *stay down*

                                        stay down

I made my blue wheels
ashamed by shouting —   *run run*

                                        run run

I set my blue wheels
to still and jet —   *come'ere*

                                        come'ere

I felt my blue wheels
kick kick —   *not yet not yet*

                                              not yet not yet

I let my blue wheels
hate hate —   *we were always late*

                                              we were always late

I gave my blue wheels
a cradle to raid —   *now spill the mouth*

                                              now spill the mouth

30

I left my blue wheels
a turn to rule —   *go mule the bed*

                                   go mule the bed

I closed my blue wheels
my fast my faster —   *time the timer*

                                   don't time the timer

I backed my blue wheels
a turn of tirades —   *ups-a-daisy*

                                   ups-a-daisy

I rolled my blue wheels
the run they wanted —   *let down your money*

                                   man, let it down

I said my blue wheels
would rise rise —   *wrong wrong*

                                   I was wrong wrong

I thought my blue wheels
could save the ocean —   *metal metal*

                                   metal metal

I gave my blue wheels
the rest they needed —   *now spill the rounding*

                                   now run the mouth

I told my blue wheels

to wait —   *break*

                             break

TO THE THINGS WE NAME

harmonics extend

over colored attenuations

       flanged opulent circumference miser

       cruxed

       flowed

       mantel hoarder

to create from a mistake

. . . of what   logic

               spirit

               etheric   . . . ?

               define

               mistake

               as the one

               that defines you   this is

                                   — WE —

                                   inside

                                   the

                                   grand

                                   WE

                                   of

                                   THINGS

CHAOS IS A FLOWER

FROM ''A BOOK OF QUESTIONS FOR THE PALINDROMIC YEAR''

The first palindromic number is 11. The palindromic years of my lifetime have given me my palindromic birth years. In 1991, I was 33 years old . . . 11 years later in 2002, I'll be 44 years old—a phenomenological occurrence worthy of exchange, at this point in my cycle. My Reversal Year will now give way to my Extra Year, which is what I've chosen to name this immediate evolution, happening in one swift charge, an 11-year clip at one fell swoop. I have lived as a 33-year-old for many years. Adding both numbers, I have carried on like a six-year-old, and I expect it's now time to act like an eight-year-old. Though by the time this story is published, I will have aged exponentially for what I imagine will be the next eleven years, or ten, losing the one extra year in the palindromic cycle, my 55th into my 66th, etc.—picture a year in apparition, as a rogue in search of its leap.

The One Year was born and went its lifetime looking to be inserted into someone's life. An only year, the One Year buzzed in and out of humanity's hive, granting someone an Extra Year, taken out of someone else's life. With no competition, the One Year wished to be the Extra Year instead. Trapped by its function to begin, the wish inserted itself by way of palindrome—fooling One into becoming New instead of Extra. Now One appeared as desire. While Extra waited for revival—asking, who wants to be new, *anything but new*, shiny newness is the first to get stepped on.

Eleven years later I revert to ten, at the time of this reading—to continue my palindromic cycle. Is this my Extra Year? In this, my Extra Year, have I met whom I've taken this year from? When I next shake your hand, will I be looking into the eye of an extra year? In that glimmer of sleep, you may find yours. When I see you next, remind me of where I was, or if it's your job, where I am going. This portal closes quick and limits exchange, but I am monstrously proportioned for expectation. The burden seems to overwhelm, but the connection is inevitable. This is offering you palindromes out there, a lifetime of possessions in my head. But palindromic lifetimes are a dime-a-dozen-nezo-daem-id . . . and I expect this liberty too, shall pass.

New became Old quickly and now, an Older Newness has prevailed over the New Old Order. There are now countries standing in line, waiting for this New Oldness. A controlled Oldness cultivated by Chaos. If we restructure the word Chaos and plant it, so it can sprout amongst itself, the Old Newness will get recultivated. However, the New Oldness will never co-exist with itself, it's got to fold into its own field. A field of letters replanted as flowers. For in this reconstruction of the word Chaos, it's been exposed for what it really is. Chaos is a flower.

A poppy . . .
Barefoot in the moon
Saying bye bye to the sky
Saying hi hi to the day
In the bloom
Of barefoot poppies . . .

You search an entire year for a time you were New, a speed forever out of direction. Trapped in its formulant wings, a New Oldness lets a translucent day unfurl an entire year as one instant. And this one, right now, has just occurred. And here I cast it frozen in print—on the third day of my Extra Year I've taken my pen and laid out the beginnings of a promise. And on this, the 44th day, I've killed it, needing to travel light. And on the 55th day, One came down and asked me what I wanted. And on this, the 22nd day, I was unprepared—but after I go through you, I'll know what I want, said the palindromic yob looking at his reflection.

35

And here, on the 77th day, I ask you, asking me—who needs to travel light in a year of reversal? Surrounded by no possessions, I am home. Missing my pinkie ring, its replacement waits for me this year. Losing it is a mark for change—I am searching for my next year to wear on my finger. A band of metal to encircle my skin. No power to it, no morality, no vanity—just a ring. A marker of time identifying its arrival. Possession-as-Passassion—surrounded by passion, I am most at home in my head. A lifetime of possessions in my head, their access still renews. The sum total of each palindrome is renewed by the year of its arrival. This year equals 4. The last one equals 20. Take each one in history. The sum total is always even, but this is too easy. Better to take your Extra Year and say what was done with that time. Loudly. In a room without openings. Surrounded by possessions. Reinvention as the master of sound or dnuos for etsam.

To relate the palindromic tendency to your world, filter every occurrence through your personal history. For example, there's the matter of the palindromic date. Falling on the 33rd day of the palindromic year. Which was the 33rd anniversary of my father's death. This is not fiction. He was taken on an icy road on Feb. 2, 1969. They say he always worked late. They also say he was misguided, and allowed luxury a place at the table, and that his children were always first, and that his son would reinvent an extra year on this date. Or on the accumulated histories attached to this date. I am looking to assure his continuity through my palindromic son—the Third one born by the First one reborn as the Extra one.

A palindrome assures continuity—the entry into itself reborn at every passing. By becoming itself in the course of its lifetime, palindromes are the most human words. A palindrome reminds itself that, in the end, it is still alive, still there by going backwards. This year will be here, still, as a comment on every year. Age moves forward stepping through time emit hguorht gnippets.

It is the first palindromic year. Chaos is a flower in my head. The bees of humanity buzz about me in their glorious stink. It is eleven years from now. Stepping back or forward. Here in the hills of Chaos. Terrains of Discovery reverse themselves. Lifts of weed grow ten miles long. Blades of grass grow ten miles long. They take turns growing into and out of each other. Here in the hills of Chaos there is no trash or waste, just Chaos. As far as the eye can see, can you? Chaos is a flower. In a field of poppies . . .

> *Papi, papi / Tell me how I'm gonna grow*
> *Tell me how I'm gonna stand like you do*
> *Tell me how I'm gonna stretch like you do*
> *Tell me how I'm gonna be just like you, o-oh . . .*
> *Mami, Mami / Tell me how I'm gonna grow*
> *Tell me how I'm gonna dance like you do*
> *Tell me how I'm gonna dream like you do*
> *Tell me how I'm gonna be just like you, o-oh . . .*

I, as palindromic yob, stand as I. Aware of my people, moving as I. Placed in the order of my missing I. Submerged in the slope's determined slant, gaining on my last name, a speed forever out of my grasp. My last name impossibly un-palindromic. My instants reborn in the crossfire. My reincarnations ready for I.

What my extra year will bring to someone I haven't met is the prospect of extra time. The desire for time is deeper for someone who cheats desire, who rubs from their skin an extra layer of time. This is another start, to find where *extra* ends. To state plainly the one extra moment of *day*. That is, to *else* the earlier chance of numbers, where years reverse, back at the beginning of this writing. Useful now, at the end of this writing, in this multiplication of *skin* over human word—clarity in exchange for clarity's understanding.

I saw a man wearing my shirt today, he was my brother but holding not my brother. How men say *brother* but really mean gender. Is my gender enough to be home? Half my planet is home. Is year a home? Can year find a home on this planet? A time once found itself to be time and made itself a home. Half-time is home. The other half is gender.

When walking through your preordained doors, listen for the frictive rub. This starting to stop and back, this constant travel, noisy in the right light, is endlessly reversal's opposite— and, according to your year, replaces what door you walk through. Barefoot, about goal and arrival, about creating once you've landed. In the instant of *renewness*, chaos is attractive. Language words as hills, passing back and forth over themselves. This is the instant of itself at home. The palindromic yob loses sih edam-fles at yreve tnatsni.

> *Cover me now*
> *My blue fated draper*
> *Date mating undertaker*
> *My blued over-robed coverer*
> *Cover me now . . .*

This was a boy. A small one of me. Made this instant. From a talk of my own. With someone. Maybe me. This boy was a talking of someone. Made to fit. In my mouth. My mind. This instant was a boy. Running in place. Saying, I had to have been this once, in my mouth. I haven't met you yet. But I am sure you will meet my time. The one I made with my extra year.

(NOTE: THIS BEGAN IN 1991 WAS RESUMED IN 2002
AND WILL BE COMPLETED IN 2112—ETORRESERROTE)

TOPOGRAPHY FOR
THE UNINITIATED

now that I let myself look for you
I need you to tell me
how to move when I'm wrong —

you know, that place
where I separate youth
from whatever it is I am now

— peel back, inspect the fringes
of your recalcitrant wake — is what I would say
to someone stepping through privacy

who knows how to talk
to an empty vessel — is one answer —
who can pretend that a trail

knows its outcome
a seeable future, ignited
by a spirit's past —

I gave you a poem, it was for you
to give back — do you remember now
what it is you owe me

a lion cub's albino foreskin
something I can't touch
leave anything alone

the right person will discover when to look
— there was no one who needed these words
receiver matched to message

the nothing facade
hidden within faith and feature
— please, do we talk now

or is that the idea
to leave things alone
until they talk back

AURORA'S AURA

Just don't see your reason your idea,
if this means I go without your theory
your moment, let me fly without your warmth
your embrace, but if this leaves me spent
without your tongue your touch,
I'd rather stay without your mandate
your manifesto, and crawl inside your nut
your hole, for I could never stomach your pity
your apathy, without your knowledge
your information, attending your synopsis
your reach, your overarching timbre
your tone, of which I've become enamored
possessed, to the point where all my reason
my want, intended for fulfillment
for breeding, has colored this encounter
this summit, with so much indecision
persuasion, without your empty statement
your pointing, correcting my alignment
my talking, I'd tackle all your diction
your throneing, and make you answer wrongings
and spokens, but here we've shook our hands
our fingers, and given each a lecture
a gassing, so after all this molding
this preaching, I have to say with focus

with fizzle, that if I'd been your savior
your Jesus, we never would have fisted
not fighted, you left me no surrender
no choice, to mangle your direction
your essay, so let's agree to listen
to leave, each other without heartbreak
without distance, I leave you with your theory
your reason, don't ever try to call me
don't email, we'll never have our childhood
our Paris, without you there's no envy
no wanting, antagonistic virtues
withstanding, why can't I kick your habit
your knowing, I'll meet you once for coffee
for beer, we'll talk about the old days
the falsehoods, I'll challenge your inventions
your stories, you'll tell me why again.

INVERSION

circular, omnipresent, the shapes
you secrete, the ones that return

there will be ones, who keep you down
safe from their climb, faced by fear and tribulation
to dare laws of inadequacy, by turning on you
upon the times of your burn, of their bearing, upon ones
who daunt the awestruck jeers of frontal ability
with hammers of braided dilation, upon ones
who fulfill goals of inebriate dissection
tending the warmth of their callous herd, over the ones
hiding in the jackdaw, doling out magic
in the brambles that tap you

there will be ones who project beyond their fence
crediting desolation for miraculous immediacy
abandoned by structure, mozzetta of cardinal, tremor of greenery,
upon ones who will faith on the base of their reign
to lord in the heavens what counts for one day
crossing, one over the other, the loudness of their revolving sucre,
buried and raw in the pindots, drained across their own planes,
constellations, cleared of their own connections
by the ones at the edge, the ones who shape the objects
that continue without you

SOLSTICE

I surround the immediate light
gathered for what seems like a glimmer
at you and me — looking at each other
right here

and I'm asking you to step in
to awaken the scars of our hands
as early reminders — folding into our names
I'm trying to remember

the immediate flesh
what we call things that belong
once they age — as if earth could wear
the spots we stand in

the observed available
the you and I we impression by flesh —
a fleeting instant that grows
from the edges of things we try to name

OBLIQUE OFFERING

. . .

and I became the words I started with
the left alone
that never made it to my mouth my eyes
my length in conversation
with my fall my one by one
still standing
where I was

. . .

and these were the feet I found
along the broken path uncolored
by lightless night
along the white I ruined and this
was the step that called me
the one I started the left alone
that *not* became

. . .

and who was the mouth I opened
the mortal impregnation

masquerading as soul over spirit
left free by body
of wake of call of sound that left me
between traces
the world of *we* behind the one
we don't

. . .

and why did I find what *not* did
when I needed *not*
what formless occupation I invent
when I have no words just out of reach
just there, where *no* replaces *not*
for denial for meaning for sound for oblique assemblages
of higher forces that I will never see
but be

. . .

and I became the questions I asked
the incomplete arrangement
of my beauty when I started speaking
and couldn't hear my *not* speaking
my offering of *not*
a measure to leave behind
to offer my children what I was missing
and how beautifully incomplete I was

. . .

and I was to find my moves
behind me
forced to find their shadows
by the moves I took to get there
making the breath of the *get there*
be the *make* that I leave in the act
of becoming the act

SOME KINDA RIP IN WHAT I SEE

the				sucking
the				cup
the				child
the				dot
the				dot
				dot

thesucking	cup	dotdot	child	dash
the	instroke	upthecross	dotthedot	dot

you see
these things fall into a space without apology
and so do these

sidestroke				down
dashcross	brokefor	stash	dashup	slide
crossacross		swingcheck		choose
to icon		the i		dotdot

is not a god in every letter
a dream
stroke to the letter
the world as instroke up the cross is to the letter and the word
can try to better it slipper it isn't the choice of a letter
every belief you have ever had

?

You see

I see these things fall from their openings

Brokens laced together by brokens forced together

To be apart all the time I see these things

Some kinda rip in what I see

From inside the eyewell

The rip apparent

The dip into the eyelids

Torn from inside

The mouth inside the eyeball is a quiet scream dot dot slash I feel

My eyes

Into my skull

The rip apparent

From inside

What I see

You see

I'm grounded in a space that allows me

to look up at the morning sun and happily and without apology

wonder about the new day

the suckering chance

the sucking cup of child

the tentacle of child

the gouge of my eyes

fluid ink

sacs of dot

the dash of a space without apology dot dot

every icon of beauty has its vanity

every letter has its devil day

and is not every letter you have ever had some kinda involvement

some kinda dash dot stroke dash dit with

some kinda rip I'm in

some kinda ground I'm grounded in

this space trying to open

the mouth from inside the eyeball

yawning the dip into fractures

fractures

broken sky holes from inside

announcing her parrot beak elegy without apology

I

grounded in

I

allow

me

to fall

into

elegy without apology

the ground opening

the eyeball bursting

declaring

her 'ology

without apology

you see

I see these things fall apart

All the time — calling me to the rip in what I see

The suckering into wonder

                I dot dot dot but not yet

                Side stroke octamortalia

                Ink sacs of dot dot doctopi — but not yet

                      Slash

                      Pus letters dash fluid crot

                      Not but not

                      Not dot not but not

                      Not

THE ANIMAL GAME

each person picks one animal and hides it
can't be two or more than two
only one

the other person has to find the animal
and bring it to the animal circle
in the middle of the room

then there's this hand that floats over the circle
and shoots eight lasers
killing eight animals

you take those animals outside the circle
and their friends talk about them
one by one

the best friend of each animal that was killed
tells everyone in the circle
what they were like and how they miss them

after each animal talks there's this magic golden coyote
who comes up to the friend who just talked
and says abracadabra

the dead animal comes back to life
next to his friend
they all come back like this into the circle one by one

the hand is human and stretches out four by four
two times four lasers and then
eight animals die

and come back to life
born golden the coyote
is like the cow

he talks not just abracadabra he talks
like this like humans
abracadabra

at the end of the game you start again
you win
by playing the game

I WAS SO TIRED THIS MORNING
AND NOW HERE I AM AWAKE

COLLABORATION WITH KRISTIN PREVALLET

Spilled, entwined, organ'ed, zygotic, wiped, ready to receive your etcetera,
Becoming mine, etc.
Socketed each to each, chord'ed, felt-wrapped, fluid, etc.
Inched, ink't, warped, amongsted, Kriatic, impulsed, re-neutered, etc.
De-balled, un-iced, ridged prosthetics snugly fit, etc.
Neared, riddled, impossibly squandered, un-stanza'ed appreciatively, etc.
Far felt, nibbled, mouse-holed, in and out energetics, etc.

    and where does continuation happen — in the convergence
    of nouns — unattached — by no one there, anyway

    in the realm of infinite combinations: man to woman to woman to man to man
    the obliteration of bodies — the expansion of minds beyond bodies

    the obliteration of selves in the oceanic swell
    of one body arched to receive and another poised and thrusting

M'coomed, endemic . . . the moment I thought you'd finished is when I neglected to look, etc.
Overrated, the moment I thought you'd already come, etc.
Which only gave me extended notions of probe'ability, wizened circumfery, squirch, etc.

'Arch! Such zealotry tinted wisen'd your speech!
Weren't we built, impressed, and drafted upon, by squirch, by speech!
More like squelched, ensocketed, silenced by the horrors speech wrought!

    and life-affecting organisms — ungendered by motion continuers, poemers
    languagers — in the finite squirch of neurons — escape the physical

    formed of etcetera — droplets on a seed, umbilical sun enamor'd by
    rubbing of inner over inner over inner — of implausible thickness

    over aerial distance, slipped on telescopic etcetera
    of one receiver — obliterated by swell

Force of flow vastness of oceans, holes are not in opposition
Open'd the universe existenceful as
Electrons with ions collide into sound, into arch, into wave upon way,
Into sweat, saliva'd in utero, unchecked, by balm upon bone
A roam, in mindful intention of hum . . . there, what a *go*
Wants to be, like speech'd, like terror, like flamed-out etcetera

    and fleshed in the line of its ending — to curve in the time of insatiate
    deep — the propulsion of vulvivisection anon — if I

    throw myself catch me — the boy in the body to body the girl
    the oblique interruption of body parts — ground into dust by the girl

    into body the male interform — how are we not done, into the cusp
    the hold — as into the etc. the [fill me up] . . .

KABONKADONK PUTTANESCA

I) TORRES RE-EMBARRASSES TORRES AGAIN

II) TORRES FINDS CONCEPTUAL POETRY IN THE REFLECTING POOL

III) TORRES HOLDS HIS FINGERS IN HIS EARS SO HIS BRAINS DON'T FALL OUT

spent half my life on all fours

in a poem to gentrifical beginnings

in a peon to your gentle *ital*

your gentital

your gelenital	your gelentic tittle
your gelatinous eggle	your title
your jeckle	your titey
your frankenshtetl	your tite little gentleman
your go-gettal	your gentle intelligence
your getital	your jello
your general little	your telegenic junk
your galactic little jiggle	your loose change

IV) TORRES IS SO OVER

V) EDWIN YOU HAVE BEEN SELECTED BY TIME

you have been selected by time

poet Edwin Torres repositions the core of poetry.
realigns the body of poetry.
reassembles the idea of "poem." From pieces like
reassembles the body of the poem. From pieces like
poet Edwin Torres realigns the liking of.
poet Edwin Torres repositions the framework of.
poet Torres renders the framework of the possibility.
poet renders possibility.
realizes the possibility at the core of poetry.
recharges the possibility at the core of poetry.
repositions the core of the possibility of poetry.
renews the possible at the core of poetry.
"re-possibles" the possibility at the core of what is and is not poetry.
"re-possibles" the possibility of the possible.
possibly the most possible poet.
the pore of the pore.
of pore is Torres.
torn of the pore is the poet Torres.
Torres is the porn of poetry.

TO NAME THE DRAWING
YOU MUST READ IT FIRST

in both (tp) the physical and (ta) the abstract
the (ibs) in-between space is (ac) a construct

taking (mfas) many forms and shapes
(dos) drawing or speaking is a (moss) medium of shape-shifting

ideas of (odae) openness distance and entry
seem (itin) inherent to its nature for some (tib) the in-between

is a (coe) collection of essences or (pmto) prosthetic memories that overlap (aoc) audience
or canvas for others a (ni) new invention a (fisob) fabricated and implied space of being

(gaoa) geometry and allusions of architecture also appear as (ass) aural spatial systems
whereas (btib) between the in-between explores (trb) the relationship between

(ecsn) existing and constructed spaces and narratives that are shifted disoriented
and in constant flux (sdicf) (fisob) is interested in (tuoe)

the uncertainty of expressing its **(wobp)** way of being present

without **(mdfc)** making demands for completion

(tp)

(ta)

(ibsac)

(mfas)

(dos)

(moss)

(odae)

(itin)

(tib)

(coe)

(pmto)

(aoc)

(ni)

(fisob)

(gaoa)

(ass)

(btib)

(trb)

(ecsn)

(sdicf)

(fisob)

(tuoe)

(wobp)

(mdfc)

THE HAPPY SKEPTIC

Gotta background in skepticism, exposed to skepticism growin' up
given tools an'toys that tumored m'fix, y'feel me!
Preached bowls o'skeptic *love* for breakfast, every mornin'
reams worth of skeptic spat, spopped, an'squeezed that crap out, every damn cold spell.

Mastered a degree, fingered a loan outta the G.O.V.
so's I could teach it, breathe it, and puppet the coffers with some lonely *boogie pud*.
Backed up my *shimmy* with conspiracy sermons I served up, onna moving-picture show
I downloaded, to honor the fears of my family ... *no LIKE no DICE no DICE no LIKE!*

Freedom in my blood from the get-go, *got me!*
No GFE no *jefe* no shawarma daredevils. Meep meep on my molars, etched in sketch
"Skeptic 101" with CliffsNotes on my gallstones. Coyotes on a tightrope,
whistlin' alla my text messages ... to wiggle'em winners with an *inside* job, y'feel me.

Gave up, gotta high rise in 'Cino, moved in with a couple a two-timin' frauds.
You know, some status league overseas enchiladas
witta permanent hard-on for ... *watchu lookin' at* ... kidney stone alpha bits
onna fallopian fluffer? Crammin' video after video of solar flares, so's I could *pretend* ...

I'm the *right* kind of traveler, ridin' that Triple A countdown
to some punch 'n' judy macho shit ... so's I can refresh my wipe?
No can do *Mister Viva La-Gina*! Big O adolescent, *oh yeah* ... I sucked before I could bite!
Left every dive, I did my *do* in ... cleaner.

Tissue Instagram . . . *y'feel me!* Fracked chlamydia with infant clorox . . . that's right, scooped up, packed tight, and puffed every sock into my *tomatillos*, to impress them Maybelline cover-ups; little urethrans with overtwinks of mac 'n' cheese . . . I paid my rent like a MO-FO!

(BOOM) Graduated hard knocks an'freeway beeswax. (BOOM) Supported the family biz with reams of skeptic jiz. (BOOM) Flipped the bong off many a skeptic pancake. (BOOM) Jumped ship to *can't-I-squatus-land*. See my stroll on the carpet, I got me a burn the color o'Boss, wearin' my stink like a billable enema.

Subliminal nut job — best backstabber on the planet . . . the one behind you. Yeah I know . . . this is a loser talkin', hittin' the same damn walls over an'over. So tell me . . . *Mr. V* — if I ain't CLEAN and you ain't REAL . . . how come we both smell so . . . *HAPPY*?

MECCA CONFUSA:
THE T-SHIRT POEM

Allen Ginsberg, I have worn you on my back
in cafés, on the flatlands, in a threesome
with a half-stranger, whose pregnant pause stretched out
across the microcosmic corn flake of America's crooked twaddle,
your fellatious weight wigged on the temporary

munch-stains of mop-headed troubadours,
Allen Ginsberg, I wore your t-shirt with your poem
for a week in the Mediterranean heat, I was on vacation,
my luggage had been stolen, I was left wearing you on my back
unshowered, unshaved, I walked your stink

up and down those pueblo streets, looking for a remnant
of magna-cathartic putrefaction in the gutless odor of my
other t-shirts, I never washed you, too
embarrassed to reveal my scarecrow's chest
to the letters forming your exuberantly Hellenic rupture,

knowing you would have enjoyed any nipple within rim shot of
avalanche or underarm . . . with due respect . . . I endured
the sweaty lung of your mass mugged by lonely verbs, each wrinkle
a soiled verse, Allen Ginsberg, I have already written a poem, years ago,
about you, our first encounter, a peacock's tail, all sainthood sanctified

in musk and love, arising through oxidation within the cloth of our unwashed souls,
you on my back, trailing the shadow of a colorless mirror-faction by clinging
to a skinny watery funk of Puerto Rican material, far from home I exorcised
the gypsy brilliance out of your hippie-dyed tongue, earthly toad, and lay bleeding,
the green fusion of our unrequited bromance at the hooves of the peasant paparazzi,

Allen Ginsberg, I wore you for one week, and never felt your tincture
on the seemingly ghosted episode, of our mutual longing for circular oneness,
emerged in the copulating dissolution, of your entrailed alchemy < *hudda hudda*
bow bow hatsa cuoq hatsa cuoq tantric autocomaaaaaaa > a groped cigarette
smoked, from the tenements of Eisenhower's hairless nubbin

to Whitman's follicular sway of mercuric synergy, head for tail, night
for day, dogged in dualistic wet spot, moving with erectable awe
over the pigsters of your shocking grey pubis,
Allen Ginsberg, I have worn you on my back and never felt
the galactic peck of your molten po prick the rear

of America's Telemundo bypass, nor the equation of your
empatheticized mound, rip out malls and ipods from the foreign press
while wrapping your umbilical offerings across a Nintendo's worth
of whack jobs, as they beat the spores of industry into one more foreskin to cut you free,
it has now been one week of your grime, ripening down my flesh, my huge potential

immersed in the bowels of your delicate reminders, transforming meditation
from man to monk, with the iridescent wean of your burning red vibra-toot
< *consciousness liquidator borealis calibrator inbreath inbreath inbreath wasabiiiiii* >
Allen Ginsberg, your stitch count was higher, I threw away my Emily Dickinson
bedsheets, my Christian Bök umlauts and my Jack Kerouac fishnets, the day

they put my mug on Facebook and told me who I was, but I kept you because
you were made better, Allen Ginsberg t-shirt, you stood the test of time, a week's worth
of my vagrant meandering, cloaked in mandalas of sweat, in the confusion
of my tattered wolves, in a mass of unformed unicorns, and always you remained
a size too large to shrink.

SEGREGATION HAIKU

a frog family
is moving into the pond
there goes the haiku

THE THING ABOUT LATINX

O R

TO SEEK OUT THE FRAME OF
MY BODY'S ANNIHILATION
IS TO INVOKE THE ROTARION
THAT I WANT YOU TO SKIM
AND BREATHE IN

where the Latino streets
are known
the world over, as Latinx.o
　-vertaken by — .now *slash* 2 *hyphen* O *hyphen* A *hyphen* X

        i have so many left turns
        remaining — so much undiscovered hearing
        ahead of me
                Latino slash Latin@ — each nexus, left open
                    to find the human negative
                    inside the positive ‹ *the poxitive* ›

Hybrid Astrology — an alphabet i was born into

that lights my way

with .w *minus* one letter

        x as *y* — < *the Latinized version of y as x* >

< *Mxtake — Mistxke — Mistakx — which vowel replaces which crux* >

        < *try LatinX* >

la tingx . . . have we begun listening

to — *the things* — you know . . . *ex'cuchando a La Tinx*

        from deep inside the ear

    to the *x/ch/catch* — at the back of the throat —

      at the end of the x'phabet?

            as in — *used-to-be*'phabet?

< *minus the trappings of code* >

X sapien reticulation

rattling *mi gente*

— prophetic reversals

appearing along the spine

        of my most minority of M.e's

< *mi noise — be x'd — by flow* >

67

within the emerging migration — where

fractures ignite — where old pores breathe under new skin —

where post-labial confessions

get served up — between the size of a mortal

and his monument to quicksand

no longer am i — LatinO or Latin@ but LatinX

machina, makes *Ache* > at back of > *Vox.Otros*

damn *ex-paix* + Make = height.hype.I brid

— as in *vos otros* = *my kind*

making trouble again

by just showing up — x'crotic

in the scrote zone

< *Axxent on MY-nus* >

i have no solutions for no people

going nowhere — *x'curve broken heart-phabet* —

defines *definition*

as

the root of static

< *cxchxchxchxchxchxchxccxchxchxchxchcxchxchxchxchxchxchxchxchxchxchxchxchxchxch* >

a dandelion's million spores

know home more than i, the finger-released run

your *used-to-be* twist in the ear

is my *Latinized ear* — at wax with *axxent*

off the nations of my posture

lived inside your *used-to-be* control —

Damn control

Minor rage intact of

Age control

Damn Age.Damage   *< should age be your lookout >*

says 'Xicua perched on edge

< lookout for chroma re-curve

betwixted by slippage >

says 'Xtatic edged by Journey

— have i started you on yours yet, mi gente

your Xourney —

place your crux at the next turn

shout *come'ere* at the wind-borgs — multi-growing

over *molecular ethnics*

— in kinetic *kinship* of x'ed-out humans

from x'ed-out territories, born out of proportion

Xanctuary ex-Cities — crossed by action

of the *seek heating hearing*

claimed by i — a full-on *Latino Po* in x'clothing

go on, *ex* the connectors — arrange the angles of entry
— Vox Mapping 2.0
tracing outlines — that hear you back

witness America's Massive Selfie in its prime

Mi

Yo

Hexpañol

Hross í oss < *of horses and men* >

< *of mind and matter* > Hr'amicuss

Hra Hra Simil.E < *of mulch and forgiveness* >

attempting transmission at every connection — i erupt
once a century, in the tongue of my people —
approaching consumption without a flinch

< *self-carnivory — in guise of self-realm* >

go on, discuss the ravenous calm that propels an island
into its depth — write the *allowed* breath

every xyllable
existing
in i —

in dialogue of x, our xoil, fluid as tongue

i, xtongue = i, *notquite* tongue

claim to be xoet < *notquite* oet >

my x.ivilization

stretched out over your codes, O.Earth

Xglocked

& glitched — where best

to resist the zone, the crossing

sought — by X hug.o lovex ov.home

< *o blued over-robed coverer, cover me now* >

go on — Xxone xSpeak ex speakit — connect *throat* to *zone*

if my difficulty

— is in being

who i am

let me hear

— every i

claimed as *poex*

by reclaiming

island as *isla* —

a transmutable *isla* — seekin'

no border

whose *nuyo* wants me, wants this neo-boy — freshly x'ed

by mortality's run —

i resurface

at every inner coil

to speak up — to ignite the broken colony

and stand inside my talk

my x language, my *used-to-be*

'engua — knowing others

already *been'gua*

< *cryptic codes among the natives*

alive in futures already written >

— The Xicanx Xchipelago — the borders we mobilize

in every throat — Motombaxa

Xcuadorxes — hidden as native Xorixuas

ancient in their ancestral absorption — opportunity workers

under the hot Xul —

molten xcursions < *like we — you and i* >

refingering new ones, beyond the cogent

crossing over

as *i* to *dot* — as *t* to *three*

from the end

— as *x* — *y* claim another one — run — run — run

< *radical change requires radical lov.ove* >

Immigranx Xmericax

Whix Privelex

Xatino Xoet Xwin Xorres

etx. the new phrases we need — to breathe

in the run — of sounding out — connections

— to newly cracked arousals

just outside our grasp — reminders

of the speed we X language in —

right here

— at the tip of the tongue — where best to categorize defiance

but

in language

Xphabet

the *used-to-be*'phabet

ferocious

in the *Somehow* zone, Xcrete the street

before the zone —

Xxone xSpeak ex speakit

Speakit

Speakit

Speakitup

Speakitup

Speakitup

Pickitup

Pickitup

Pickitup

Pickitup

Pickitup

Pickitup

Pickitup

Pickitup

Pickitup

Pickitup

Pickitup

Pickitup

Pickitup

Pickitup

Pickitup

Pickitup

Pickitup

Pickitup . . . Los Planetas Gallopox

TOTEM

the circular body
is bound
to leave traces
at the note
of the turn

to open up the bird
that decides
when
to threaten
the undusted

how to stand under a crane?
crook the start

)W LOT ALOT
)WER THAN LOT

        ed beheaded — opening the posture
        j the mouth with booze
        r suddenly — a fish or a flesh buried by fire
        j glass ocean
        er setting rise — reads cloud as ground
        s perilous scopes engaggled
        ne choice we need
        ιange inhibition of all we crave

        on my way
        where i'm not

let me write   )f reborn opus
my cover   fixates on curve
 nd let you
 w
  ite it   will is bought
      let me write   ie seducer
    now, mmy cover   longevity of the seduced
        and let you see   ves
    ure how   ativity is a personality flaw
        i write it
                                  let me write
        you know, make   my cover
        good   and let you see
        the fissure   how
        on   i write it

reality

'hem
nside
iey if
    you can
    you know...meme meister

you know, make
good
the fissure
on
reality

them
inside
they if
    you *can*
    you know...meme meister

purity
    says image
is cloak for interruption
    says outro out of turn
sees covered sun
    runs geometric scisms to penetrate dumb
    awakens triple beta gauntlet getter to generation gun
    agoozies instability by dousing do for done

    to dingle dash
    the
    maybe-know
    that waits
    for same
    to see

    call me what i am before i know it

    terra censor *the healing portal*
    — my intersecting points of light
    arranged as a name

free will is bought
by the seducer
the longevity of the seduced
proves
creativity is a personality flaw
    there is interruption among thieves

to point at the crossroads
and see the question
— a given key to unlock it
lives inside its naming

if there
before the larger shadow
the trace grows against the grain
    then wing the step
    to absorb the corridors

    filament of apogee
    inter-symbolized moral swelter

    to question
    what you walk through
    answer your arrival
    for the footstep — to make the bringing the task
        here is a mark that has
        your name but your question
        is on this one

to point at the crossroads
and see the question
— a given key to unlock it
lives inside its naming

if there
before the larger shadow
the trace grows against the grain
    then wing the step
    to absorb the corridors

    of apogee
    ized moral swelter

    ugh
    make the bringing the task
    k that has
    your question

call it something known
so that you know it
when you leave it — give me a reminder to tell me
    my journey was memorable
    bite scrape fight fall you know…
    something to break the skin

if i cross my circle with yours
where we meet
is what comes out

BURND REBRN ABRIDG
RURN ABORN FREBRID
RAR AFRARRD REBBGGD

i was everything you asked
the not what you expect

because sun and wind reach deep inside
to call out sweet pain
pulse beyond heartbeat because
body suffers beyond its surroundings

your memory o
gets deeper, y
if you open yo
your enduran
    at e
    you
    on

if i wra
i will f

i turned a
i saw wha
i found w
my seco
i left pa
so that
the tur
gave r
all the
who i
i eve
entir
i ha
my
my
be
i'v
w
ir

the kept step
a circular asking
that knows to not land

your memory of this walk
gets deeper, you are your own imprint
if you open your taking
your endurance — you are the experiment you endure
    at every turned direction
    yours is the current you take
    on your way through your imprint

if i wrap myself in rules
i will find no self in rules

one of the noble implements impediments
of falsehood in youth
is to fall on the sword you believe in

for that making marking
in that moment
implements impediments
for that entry
outh

sword you believe in
one of the gestures
you reconcile age with
marking
is to window the spine with fluidity
it

urgently rendered
in tonal occasion
the gestures
the bearing that stands on its own
conc e age with
vindr the spine with fluidity
the circular body

is a kept one
ntly   ered
the official notice of turning
ona   ion
is to leave your traces
bf e
at stands on its own
ile

to open up the bird that decides
when to threaten the inhibition we crave

turning

traces

ird that decides
the inhibition we crave

open u
when to t
a
cross-legged
be
head
ing
in
ject
ing
th
e   stained glass ocean
moutgleems over setting rise — reads cloud as ground
h   leaves perilous scopes engaggled
wi   to water the choice we need
th
b
oo
ze

TOTEM

the circular body
is bound
to leave traces
at the note
of the turn

to open up the bird
that decides
when
to threaten
the undusted few

how to stand under a crane?
crook the start

TAKE IN — LOT A LOT A LOT
TAKE IN — LOWER THAN LOT

a cross-legged beheaded — opening the posture
                                        injecting the mouth
with time for suddenly — a fish or a flesh buried by fire
                                        stained glass ocean
gleams the setting rise — reads cloud as ground
                                        leaves perilous scopes engaggled

gonna water the choice we need —
gonna change inhibition
of all we crave —

< i'm on my way
to where i'm not >

cycle of reborn opus
orality fixates on curve

free will is bought
by the seducer
the longevity of the seduced
proves
creativity is a personality flaw

let me write
my cover
and let you see
how
i write it
you know, make good
the fissure
on
reality

to *them*
inside *they*

if
you *can*
you *know*   < *meme meister* >

purity   says image
          is cloak for interruption
          says outro out of turn
purity   sees covered sun
          runs geometric schisms to penetrate dumb
purity   awakens
          triple beta gauntlet getter
          to generation gun
agoozles   instability by dousing *do* for *done*

to *dingle-dash*
the
maybe-know
that waits
for *same*
to see

< *call me what i am before i know it* >

terra censor the healing portal
— my intersecting points of light
arranged as a name —

the boy slips on the bad word
and makes a new sentence
— the carved-out itch on land
is the new bad word

< there is interruption among thieves >

< point at the crossroads >
and see the question
— the *giving key* unlocks it
lives inside its name

if there
before the larger shadow
the trace grows against the grain
then — wing the step
to absorb the corridors

— filament of apogee
inter-symbolized moral swelter —

to question
what you walk through
answer your arrival
for the footstep — make the bringing
the task

here is a line that has
your name — but your question
is on this one

to step into the unknown
call it something known
— so you know it
when you leave it   — give me a reminder
       to tell me
       the journey was memorable —
       bite scrape fight fall
       you know . . .

       something to break the skin

if i cross my circle with yours
— where we meet
is what comes out   *— what we take*
       from
       — what comes out

BURND REBRN ABRIDG
RURN ABORN REBRID
RAR AFRARRD REBBGGD

       — i was everything you asked
       the "not what you expect"

because sun and wind reach deep inside
to call out sweat pain
pulse beyond heartbeat — because
the body suffers beyond its surroundings

your memory gets deeper
of this walk — you are your own imprint
if you open your endurance
you are the experiment you endure

at every turned direction
yours is the current you take
on your way *through* your imprint

< if i wrap myself in rules
i will find no self in rules >

i turned around on my second turn
i saw what i wasn't supposed to on my other third one
i found what i saw was me turning from before my second third one
on my fifth third one my eighth turn i left part of who i was
before i ever entered
so that all my leaving became my first turnaround
the turnarounds started to accumulate
told me a name they wanted to be known by
all the turnarounds i left at the doorway called me
who i was supposed to be and all this was before
i ever reached the point of the story where i left it all behind
entirely behind me but how can that be
i have never left it all entirely because
i'm still alive
my life being the turn i reach

my turnaround being the life i leave before i named it

before i named my life i left it

turning i gave myself i've given myself one more chance

to find a second chance where the fifth and fourth ones

are scattered by the turns i made in my life

my lives being the turns i reach at every naming, there

did you see how i left one part of my life, so i could name the other . . .

that's what i'm talking about

> — every step i give and take
> in step is taking me
> see, every time i question step
> i step — in step

> < *the kept step*
> *a circular asking that knows to not land* >

one of the noble impediments

of falsehood in youth

is to fall on the sword you believe in — for that marker

> — in that moment
> — for that entry

> one of the gestures
> you reconcile age with
> is to window the spine with fluidity

urgently rendered

in tonal occasion

the bearing that stands on its own

the circular body

is a kept one

the official notice of turning

is to leave your traces

to open up the bird that decides

when to threaten

the inhibition we crave

ACKNOWLEDGMENTS

The author would like to thank the following publications, in which these poems first appeared: **TALISMAN** — *WORD: An Anthology by A Gathering of the Tribes* (Tribes Press); **OBLIQUE OFFERING** — *Constellation* (Princeton Architectural Press); **I WAS SO TIRED THIS MORNING AND NOW HERE I AM AWAKE** — *7 Nights : 28 Poets, A Center for Book Arts 40th Anniversary Publication*; **TOPOGRAPHY FOR THE UNINITIATED** — *LiVE Mag!* 12; **ARSE POETICA** — *Tripwire* 11; **THE HAPPY SKEPTIC** — *The Recluse* 10; **THE THING ABOUT LATINX** — *The Thinx About Latinx* (The Center for Book Arts, NYC).

All slippage text and art was originally created for the Open Sessions Residency Program at The Drawing Center, NYC. slippage iv: **OCEAN OBELISK** & slippage vi: **TOTEM** were displayed in the exhibition, *Open Sessions 8: Planes and Corridors*.

Grateful thanks to Joshua Beckman for continually aligning brokens with openings, to Wave Books for your extraordinary dedication, a special shout out to the writings that appear in these pages together after sharing mutual lifetimes apart, to Elizabeth, to Rubio, to the infinite objects ahead.